B♭ CLARINET

Messiah at Christmas

GEORGE FREDERIC HANDEL

Arranged by James Curnow (ASCAP)

Order Number: CMP 1175-06-400

George Frederic Handel
Arranged by James Curnow (ASCAP)
MESSIAH AT CHRISTMAS
B♭ Clarinet

ISBN-10: 90-431-2592-X
ISBN-13: 978-90-431-2592-5

CD number: 19-089-3 CMP

GEORGE FREDERIC HANDEL

Arranged by James Curnow

Christmas Greetings!

Music at Christmas is an extremely important part of celebrating this most wonderful time of year. As we celebrate the birth of our Lord Jesus Christ, music adds much joy to the celebration.

George Frederic Handel (1685-1759) composed the entire Messiah (based on scriptural passages as arranged by Jennes) in only twenty-four days. The Christmas part of this work is generally most familiar, and more often performed, and contains a wealth of important arias and choruses that can have a tremendous impact on worship during the Christmas season.

The ten arrangements in this collection are designed to allow average to advanced players the opportunity to perform in church, school, in public or anywhere Christmas is being celebrated. As you will note, I have not used the arias and choruses in their entirety, so that their duration will better fit into a worship setting, but all of the pieces have been carefully arranged to include the original melodic content. Please refer to the scriptural references for each piece (see Contents page) during your preparation and performance of the music, as this will help you to better understand Handel's intent in creating his masterpiece of Christmas worship.

Each solo book includes an accompaniment CD which contains a sample performance of each solo, as well as the accompaniment only. This will allow the performer to practice with the accompaniment when an accompanist is not available. The accompaniment track can also be used for performances if desired. Appropriate tuning notes have been added to the compact disc recording to allow the soloist the opportunity to adjust their intonation to the intonation of the compact disc accompaniment. A separate piano accompaniment book is available.

I hope you will enjoy this addition to your Christmas celebration repertoire.

James Curnow
Composer/arranger

Contents

G.F. Handel
1. COMFORT YE
from "Messiah"

Arr. by **James Curnow** (ASCAP)

Copyright © 2006 by Curnow Music Press, Inc.

G.F. Handel
2. EV'RY VALLEY SHALL BE EXALTED
from "Messiah"

Arr. by **James Curnow** (ASCAP)

G.F. Handel
3. AND THE GLORY OF THE LORD
from "Messiah"

Track

Arr. by **James Curnow** (ASCAP)

G.F. Handel
5. O THOU THAT TELLEST GOOD TIDINGS TO ZION
from "Messiah"

Track

Arr. by **James Curnow** (ASCAP)

G.F. Handel
6. FOR UNTO US A CHILD IS BORN
from "Messiah"

Arr. by **James Curnow** (ASCAP)

Arr. by **James Curnow** (ASCAP)

Track
15 16

8. REJOICE GREATLY, O DAUGHTER OF ZION

G.F. Handel

from "Messiah"

Arr. by **James Curnow** (ASCAP)

Track

Rall.

G.F. Handel

9. HE SHALL FEED HIS FLOCK LIKE A SHEPHERD

from "Messiah"

Arr. by **James Curnow** (ASCAP)

10. HALLELUJAH CHORUS

G.F. Handel

from "Messiah"

Arr. by **James Curnow** (ASCAP)

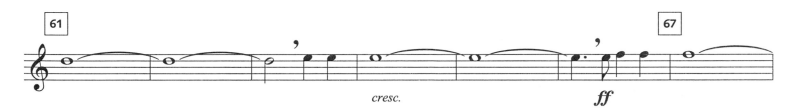

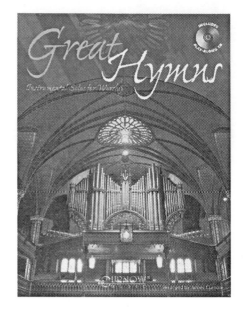

Arranged by James Curnow (ASCAP)

GREAT HYMNS

For this book, James Curnow skillfully arranged a number of world-famous hymns and chorales. On the CD are two tracks per title: the first features the melody; the second track only features the accompaniment. Contents: *All Creatures of Our God and King • Praise to the Lord • The Almighty • Be Thou My Vision • Joyful, Joyful • We Are Three Brethren* and more.

Flute / Oboe / Violin	CMP 0354-00-400
Bb Clarinet / Bb Tenor Saxophone	CMP 0355-00-400
Eb Alto Saxophone	CMP 0356-00-400
F Horn or Eb Horn	CMP 0351-00-400
Bb Trumpet	CMP 0357-00-400
Trombone / Euphonium BC/TC / Bassoon	CMP 0358-00-400
Piano / Organ Accompaniment	CMP 0359-00-401

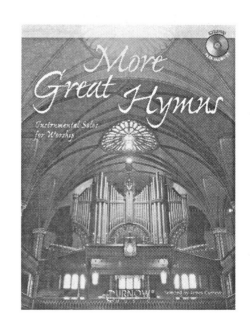

Arranged by James Curnow (ASCAP)

MORE GREAT HYMNS

Following the footsteps of GREAT HYMNS, MORE GREAT HYMNS contains ten well-known hymns from around the world. These arrangements can be performed either with the accompaniment CD (included in the solo book) or with Piano accompaniment. Contents: Amazing Grace, Easter Glory, Holy God, We Praise Thy Name, Holy, Holy, Holy, How Firm a Foundation, Jesu, Joy of Man's Desiring, Lead On, O King Eternal, My Faith Looks Up to Thee, O For a Thousand Tongues to Sing, and Softly and Tenderly.

Flute / Oboe / Mallet Percussion	CMP 0927-04-400
Bb Clarinet / Bb Bass Clarinet	CMP 0928-04-400
Eb Alto Saxophone	CMP 0929-04-400
Bb Trumpet	CMP 0930-04-400
F Horn or Eb Horn	CMP 0931-04-400
Trombone / Euphonium BC/TC / Bassoon	CMP 0932-04-400
Piano / Organ Accompaniment	CMP 0933-04-401

Arranged by James Curnow (ASCAP)

GREAT CAROLS

GREAT CAROLS is a collection of some of the world's greatest Christmas carols, delightfully arranged in fresh settings by some of the foremost composers in the instrumental field. This product is specifically designed to be flexible by the inclusion of optional cued notes, allowing the performer to choose the difficulty level that is appropriate for them. The accompaniment CD (included in the solo book) provides a demonstration performance of each solo. It also allows the soloist to practice or perform with the CD when an accompanist is not available. Capture the very essence of Christmas as you perform these arrangements of GREAT CAROLS.

Flute / Oboe / Mallet Percussion	CMP 0835-03-400
Bb Clarinet / Bb Tenor Saxophone	CMP 0836-03-400
Eb Alto Saxophone	CMP 0837-03-400
Bb Trumpet	CMP 0833-03-400
F Horn or Eb Horn	CMP 0839-03-400
Trombone / Euphonium BC/TC / Bassoon	CMP 0838-03-400
Piano / Organ Accompaniment	CMP 0834-03-401

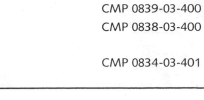

George Frederic Handel
Arranged by James Curnow (ASCAP)

MESSIAH AT EASTER

Music at Easter is an extremely important part of celebrating this wonderful time of year. As we celebrate the resurrection of our Lord Jesus Christ, music adds much joy to the celebration.

Though the Christmas part of the Messiah by Georg Frederic Handel is generally most familiar, and more often performed, the Easter portion contains a wealth of important arias and choruses that can have a tremendous impact on worship during the Easter season.

The ten arrangements in this collection are designed to allow average to advanced players the opportunity to perform in church, school, in public or anywhere Easter is being celebrated.

Each solo book includes an accompaniment CD which contains a sample performance of each solo, as well as the accompaniment only. This will allow the performer to practice with the accompaniment when an accompanist is not available. The accompaniment track can also be used for performances if desired. A separate piano accompaniment book is available.

1. Lift Up Your Heads
2. How Beautiful Are the Feet
3. Their Sound Has Gone Out
4. I Know That My Redeemer Liveth
5. Since By Man Came Death
6. The Trumpet Shall Sound
7. O Death Where Is Thy Sting and But Thanks Be To God
8. If God Before Us
9. Worthy Is The Lamb
10. Hallelujah Chorus

Flute / Oboe / Mallet Percussion	CMP 1184-06-400
Bb Clarinet	CMP 1185-06-400
Eb Alto Saxophone	CMP 1186-06-400
Bb Trumpet	CMP 1187-06-400
F Horn / Eb Horn	CMP 1188-06-400
Trombone / Euphonium BC/TC / Bassoon	CMP 1189-06-400
Piano / Organ Accompaniment	CMP 1190-06-400

CURNOW
MUSIC